D1281275

POETRY AND DRAMA

The Theodore Spencer Memorial Lecture

NOVEMBER 21, 1950

T. S. ELIOT

POETRY AND DRAMA

HARVARD UNIVERSITY PRESS · CAMBRIDGE, MASSACHUSETTS

nineteen fifty-one

POETRY AND DRAMA

IT IS A CUSTOMARY ACT OF RESPECT that the lecturer on a foundation should begin by saying something about the man in whose name the lectureship was founded. On the present occasion there are two strong reasons why this reminder should be more than the ordinary formal tribute. This is the first of the lectures to be given annually in the name of Theodore Spencer, sometime Boylston Professor of Rhetoric in Harvard University. In the second place, the fact that between Theodore Spencer and myself there had been a long friendship, terminated only by death, was, I believe, the primary reason for my being asked to inaugurate this series — as it was certainly my primary reason for accepting the honour. If I speak of him at greater length than is usual on such occasions, I feel sure that you will not only excuse but approve my doing so. There must be many of his friends and former pupils in this audience; much that I shall say of him will therefore be familiar knowledge; but I am sure that an act of homage to his personality, his work, and his influence will be welcome to all of you.

Except when there has been some accident to fix it in my memory, I find that I seldom remember the occasion of my first meeting with anyone who has subsequently become an associate or friend. I am not now sure whether I first met Theodore Spencer while he was an undergraduate at Trinity College, Cambridge, or on some later visit that he paid to England — for he loved Cambridge and liked to return there. I had certainly met him in England, and probably several times, before I came to Harvard as Norton Professor in 1932. But it was during that year, when I saw him almost every day, at Eliot House, or in his own home, or in the company of mutual friends, that we were closely associated; and it was through this constant frequentation that I came to love and appreciate the man. He put his time most generously at my disposal; helped me at every juncture with a course of lectures to a small class which he himself had been instrumental in selecting; and there was no detail of daily life in which he was not ready to give aid, and no material need which he was not anxious to anticipate. And the day on which he did not drop in for a chat before lunch was always a duller day than the others.

After 1933 I saw him, of course, only at intervals. He visited England several times — I remember that he was present, in Cambridge, at the Congregation at which I received a doctor's degree, and I remember his pleasure in the event. Between visits, we carried on a desultory correspondence. In 1938, or perhaps early in 1939, the rumour reached us in England that economies were being effected which might be adverse to his promotion or security of tenure in this university; and I was a party to the manoeuvres of some of his friends in Cambridge, England, toward obtaining for him a lectureship there. You know that he was in 1939 appointed to a lectureship at Cambridge University, but that, owing to the outbreak of war, the immediate reduction in the numbers of students in the English Tripos (for only those were left who were unfit for wartime service), and the consequent reduction in the number of tutors, it was deemed best that his appointment should be deferred. This was a great disappointment to his friends in England; but, on the other hand, we had the pleasure of hearing of his reappointment to Harvard as "visiting lecturer from Cambridge University." It was not long before he received promotion.

I should like to add a note which I hope is not indiscreet. When the august position of Boylston Professor became vacant, Ted Spencer was not one to covet that post for himself. He wrote to me privately, to ask whether I would consider the position if my name were put forward. Well, there were several reasons, both private and public, why I could not regard myself as eligible: not the least of which was my lack of scholarship — I think I told him that I should have had to spend all my spare time reading the books I ought to have read, and would have no leisure left for writing. My delight and satisfaction were great when

I read that he himself had received that distinguished appointment.

Though I do not remember our first meeting, I remember very clearly our last. It was in Cambridge, Massachusetts, just before my return to London, and only a few weeks before his death. He was full of enthusiasm for the work he was to undertake that year; he appeared in better health, and more radiantly happy, than I had ever seen him; and I thought that he had many years of both scholarly and creative work and of useful influence before him.

I do not need to remind those who knew him, or indeed those who were even slightly acquainted with him, of the charm of his personality, his interest in human beings, his gaiety, sense of humour, and conviviality — with a bearing such that he could put his pupils on terms of informal equality, without ever losing his dignity or their respect. He had several traits, in happy combination, which made him a good teacher. His standards of scholarship were high, and his view of English studies was humane; he mixed with men of letters in New York and London, as well as in the universities; he was perfectly at ease in society, whether intellectual society or not, so that he knew his students as human beings, not merely as candidates for degrees. He had a sensitive appreciation of the best in contemporary literature; and his own poetic gift was genuine. His poetry had developed, and would I believe have gone on to still greater strength after he had further assimilated and re-created the powerful influence of Yeats. But I have left to the last, mention of those characteristics which most endeared him as a friend: humility, charity, generosity, and what I can only call a fundamental goodness.

In choosing a subject for this lecture, I have had in mind, first, that it should be a subject in some way related to Theodore Spencer's interests, second, that it should be a subject on which he himself would have liked to hear me speak, and third, that it should be a subject about which this audience might like to hear me speak. Poetic drama was certainly something that Spencer cared about: I hardly need to mention his studies of Shakespeare, or his fascinated interest in the poetry of Shakespeare's contemporaries; but I should like to remind you of those performances of Elizabethan drama by the members of Eliot House which Spencer did so much to inspire and organize and in which he participated with so much zest (I remember in particular a performance of *The Shoemaker's Holiday* in which the late Master, Roger Merriman, played the part of the King with all the majesty appropriate to the Master of a Harvard House). As for myself, this is no new subject for me; in fact, reviewing my critical output for the last thirty-odd years, I am surprised to find how constantly I have returned to the drama, whether by examining the work of the contemporaries of Shakespeare, or by reflecting on the possibilities of the future. It may even be that people are weary of hearing me on this subject. But, while I find that I have been composing variations on this theme all my life, my views have been continually modified and renewed by increasing experience; so that I am impelled to take stock of the situation afresh at every stage of my own experimentation. And I hope that I have profited by this experience.

As I have gradually learned more about the problems of poetic drama, and the conditions which it must fulfill if it is to justify itself, I have made a little clearer to myself, not only my own reasons for wanting to write in this form, but the more general reasons for wanting to see it restored to its place. And I think that if I say something about these problems and conditions, it should make clearer to other people whether and, if so, why poetic drama has anything potentially to offer the playgoer that prose drama cannot. For I start with the assumption that if poetry is merely a decoration, an added embellishment, if it merely gives people of literary tastes the pleasure of listening to poetry at the same time that they are witnessing a play, then it is superfluous. It must justify itself dramatically, and not merely be fine poetry shaped into a dramatic form. From this it follows that no play should be written in verse for which prose is *dramatically* adequate. And from this it follows, again, that the audience, its attention held by the dramatic action, its emotions stirred by the situation between the characters, should be too intent upon the play to be wholly conscious of the medium.

Whether we use prose or verse on the stage, they are both but means to an end. The difference, from one point of view, is not so great as we might think. In those prose plays which survive, which are read and produced on the stage by later generations, the prose in which the characters speak is as remote, for the best part, from the vocabulary, syntax, and rhythm of our ordinary speech — with its fumbling for words, its constant recourse to approximation, its disorder and its unfinished sentences — as verse is. Like verse, it has been written, and rewritten. Our two greatest prose stylists in the drama — apart from Shakespeare and the other Elizabethans who mixed prose and verse in the same play — are, I believe, Congreve and Bernard Shaw. A speech by a character of Congreve or of Shaw has — however clearly the characters may be differen-tiated — that unmistakable personal rhythm which is the mark of a prose style, and of which only the most accomplished conversationalists — who are for that matter usually monologuists — show any trace in their talk. We have all heard (too often!) of Molière's character who expressed surprise when told that he spoke prose. But it was M. Jourdain who was right, and not his mentor or his creator: he did not speak prose — he only talked. For I mean to draw a triple distinction: between prose, and verse, and our ordinary speech which is mostly below the level of either verse or prose. So if you look at it in this way, it will appear that prose, on the stage, is as artificial as verse: or alternatively, that verse can be as natural as prose. But while the sensitive member of the audience will appreciate, when he hears fine prose spoken in a play, that this is something better than ordinary conversation, he does not regard it as a wholly different language from that which he himself speaks, for that would interpose a barrier between himself and the imaginary characters on the stage. Too many people, on the other hand, approach a play which they know to be in verse, with the consciousness of the difference. It is unfortunate when they are repelled by verse, but it can also be deplorable when they are attracted by verse — if that means that they are prepared to enjoy the play and the language of the play as two separate things. The chief effect and style and rhythm in dramatic speech, whether it be in prose or verse, should be unconscious.

From this it follows that a mixture of prose and verse in the same play is generally to be avoided: each transition makes the auditor aware, with a jolt, of the medium. It is, we may say, justifiable when the author wishes to produce this jolt: when, that is, he wishes to transport the audience violently from one plane of reality to another. I suspect that this kind of transition was easily acceptable to an Elizabethan audience, to whose ears both prose and verse came naturally; who liked highfalutin and low comedy in the same play; and to whom it seemed perhaps proper that the more humble and rustic characters should speak in a homely language, and that those of more exalted rank should rant in verse. But even in the plays of Shakespeare some of the prose passages seem to be designed for an effect of contrast which, when achieved, is something that can never become old-fashioned. The knocking at the gate in *Macbeth* is an example that comes to everyone's mind; but it has long seemed to me that the alternation of scenes in prose with scenes in verse in *Henry IV* points an ironic contrast between the world of high politics and the world of common life. The audience probably thought they were getting their accustomed chronicle play garnished with amusing scenes of low life; yet the prose scenes of both Part I and Part II provide a sardonic comment upon the bustling ambitions of the chiefs of the parties in the insurrection of the Percys.

Today, however, because of the handicap under which verse drama suffers, I believe that prose should be used very sparingly indeed; that we should aim at a form of verse in which everything can be said that has to be said; and that when we find some situation which is intractable in verse, it is merely that our form of verse is inelastic. And if there prove to be scenes which we cannot put in verse, we must either develop our verse, or avoid having to introduce such scenes. For we have to accustom our audiences to verse to the point at which they will cease to be conscious of it; and to introduce prose dialogue would only be to distract their attention from the play itself to the medium of its expression. But if our verse is to have so wide a range that it can say anything that has to be said, it follows that it will not be "poetry" all the time. It will only be "poetry" when the dramatic situation has reached such a point of intensity that poetry becomes the natural utterance, because then it is the only language in which the emotions can be expressed at all.

It is indeed necessary for any long poem, if it is to escape monotony, to be able to say homely things without bathos, as well as to take the highest flights without sounding exaggerated. And it is still more important in a play, especially if it is concerned with contemporary life. The reason for writing even the more pedestrian parts of a verse play in verse instead of prose is, however, not only to avoid calling the audience's attention to the fact that it is at other moments listening to poetry. It is also that the verse rhythm should have its effect upon the hearers, without their being conscious of it. A brief analysis of one scene of Shakespeare's may illustrate this point. The opening scene of *Hamlet* — as well constructed an opening scene as that of any play ever written — has the advantage of being one that everybody knows.

What we do not notice, when we witness this scene in the theatre, is the great variation of style. Nothing is superfluous, and there is no line of poetry which is not justified by its dramatic value. The first twenty-two lines are built of the simplest words in the most homely idiom. Shakespeare had worked for a long time in the theatre, and written a good many plays, before reaching the point at which he could write those twenty-two lines. There is nothing quite so simplified and sure in his previous work. He first developed conversational, colloquial verse in the monologue of the character part — Faulconbridge in *King John*, and later the Nurse in *Romeo and Juliet*. It was a much further step to carry it unobtrusively into the dialogue of brief replies. No poet has begun to master dramatic verse until he can write lines which, like these in *Hamlet*, are *transparent*. You are consciously attending, not to the poetry, but to the meaning of the poetry. If you were hearing *Hamlet* for the first time, without knowing anything about the play, I do not think that it would occur to you to ask whether the speakers were speaking in verse or prose. The verse is having a different effect upon us from prose; but, at the moment, what we are aware of is the frosty night, the officers keeping watch on the battlements, and the foreboding of an ominous action. I do not say that there is no place for the situation in which part of one's pleasure will be the enjoyment of hearing beautiful poetry — providing that the author gives it, in that place, dramatic inevitability. And of course, when we have both seen a play several times and read it between performances, we begin to analyse the means by which the author has produced his effects. But in the immediate impact of this scene we are unconscious of the medium of its expression.

From the short, brusque ejaculations at the beginning, suitable to the situation and to the character of the guards — but not expressing more character than is required for their function in the play — the verse glides into a slower movement with the appearance of the courtiers Horatio and Marcellus.

Horatio says 'tis but our fantasy . . .

and the movement changes again on the appearance of Royalty, the ghost of the King, into the solemn and sonorous

What art thou, that usurp'st this time of night . . .

(and note, by the way, this anticipation of the plot conveyed by the use of the verb *usurp*); and majesty is suggested in a reference reminding us whose ghost this is:

> *So frown'd he once, when, in an angry parle,*
> *He smote the sledded Polacks on the ice.*

There is an abrupt change to staccato in Horatio's words to the Ghost on its second appearance; this rhythm changes again with the words

> *We do it wrong, being so majestical,*
> *To offer it the show of violence;*
> *For it is, as the air, invulnerable,*
> *And our vain blows malicious mockery.*

The scene reaches a resolution with the words of Marcellus:

> *It faded on the crowing of the cock.*
> *Some say that ever 'gainst that season comes*
> *Wherein our Saviour's birth is celebrated,*
> *The bird of dawning singeth all night long . . .*

and Horatio's answer:

> *So have I heard and do in part believe it.*
> *But, look, the morn, in russet mantle clad,*
> *Walks o'er the dew of yon high eastern hill.*
> *Break we our watch up. . .*

This is great poetry, and it is dramatic; but besides being poetic and dramatic, it is something more. There emerges, when we analyse it, a kind of musical design also which reinforces and is one with the dramatic movement. It has checked and accelerated the pulse of our emotion without our knowing it. Note that in these last words of Marcellus there is a deliberate brief emergence of the poetic into consciousness. When we hear the lines

> *But, look, the morn, in russet mantle clad,*
> *Walks o'er the dew of yon high eastern hill*

we are lifted for a moment beyond character, but with no sense of unfitness in the words coming, and at this moment, from the lips of Horatio. The transitions in the scene obey laws of the music of dramatic poetry. Note that the two lines of Horatio which I have quoted twice are preceded by a line of the simplest speech which might be either verse or prose:

> *So have I heard and do in part believe it*

and that he follows them abruptly with a half line which is hardly more than a stage direction:

> *Break we our watch up.*

It would be interesting to pursue, by a similar analysis, this problem of the double pattern in great poetic drama — the pattern which may be examined from the point of view of stagecraft or from that of the music. But I think that the examination of this one scene is enough to show us that verse is not merely a formalisation, or an added decoration, but that it intensifies the drama. It should indicate also the importance of the unconscious effect of the verse upon us. And lastly, I do not think that this effect is felt only by those members of an audience who "like poetry" but also by those who go for the play alone. By the people who do not like poetry, I mean those who cannot sit down with a book of poetry and enjoy reading it: these people also, when they go to a play in verse, should be affected by the poetry. And these are the audiences whom the writer of such a play ought to keep in mind.

At this point I might say a word about those plays which we call *poetic,* though they are written in prose. The plays of John Millington Synge form rather a special case, because they are based upon the idiom of a rural people whose speech is naturally poetic, both in imagery and in rhythm. I believe that he even incorporated phrases which he had heard from these country people of Ireland. The language of Synge is not available except for plays set among that same people. We can draw more general conclusions from the plays in prose, so much admired in my youth and now hardly even read, by Maeterlinck. These plays are in a different way restricted in their subject matter; and to say that the characterisation in them is dim is an understatement. I do not deny that they have some poetic quality. But in order to be poetic in prose, a dramatist has to be so consistently poetic that his scope is very limited. Synge wrote plays about characters whose originals in life talked poetically, so he could make them talk poetry and remain real people. The poetic-prose dramatist who has not this advantage has to be too poetic. The poetic drama in prose is more limited by poetic convention, or by our conventions as to what subject matter is poetic, than is the poetic drama in verse. A really dramatic verse can be employed, as Shakespeare was able to employ it, to say the most matter-of-fact things.

Yeats is a very different case from Maeterlinck or Synge. A study of his development as a dramatist would show, I think, the great distance he went, and the triumph of his last plays. In his first period, he wrote plays in verse about subjects conventionally accepted as suitable for verse, in a metric which — though even at that early stage having the personal Yeats rhythm — is not really a form of speech quite suitable for anybody except mythical kings and queens. His middle-period *Plays for Dancers* are very beautiful indeed, but they do not solve any problem for the dramatist in verse: they are poetic prose plays with important interludes in verse. It was only in his last play *Purgatory* that he solved his problem of speech in verse, and laid all his successors under obligation to him.

Now, I am going to venture to make some observations based on my own experience, which will lead me to comment on my intentions, failures, and partial successes, in my own plays. I do this in the belief that any explorer or experimenter in new territor may, by putting on record a kind of journal of his xplorations, say something of use to those who f ɔw him into the same regions and who will perhaps ɔo further.

The first thing of any importance that I discovered was that a writer who has worked for years, and achieved some success, in writing other kinds of verse, has to approach the writing of a verse play in a different frame of mind from that to which he has been accustomed in his previous work. In writing other verse, I think that one is writing, so to speak, in terms of one's own voice: the way it sounds when you read it to yourself is the test. For it is yourself speaking. The question of communication, of what the reader will get from it, is not paramount: if your poem is right to you, you can only hope that the readers will eventually come to accept it. The poem can wait a little while; the approval of a few sympathetic and judicious critics is enough to begin with; and it is for future readers to meet the poet more than halfway. But in the theatre, the problem of communication presents itself immediately. You are deliberately writing verse for other voices, not for your own, and you do not know whose voices they will be. You are aiming to write lines which will have an immediate effect upon an unknown and unprepared audience, to be interpreted to that audience by unknown actors rehearsed by an unknown producer. And the unknown audience cannot be expected to show any indulgence towards the poet. The poet cannot afford to write his play merely for his admirers, those who know his non-dramatic work and are prepared to receive favourably anything he puts his name to. He must write with an audience in view which knows nothing and cares nothing about any previous success he may have had before he ventured into the theatre. Hence one finds out that many of the things one likes to do, and knows how to do, are out of place; and that every line must be judged by a new law, that of dramatic relevance.

When I wrote *Murder in the Cathedral* I had the advantage for a beginner of an occasion which called for a subject generally admitted to be suitable for verse. Verse plays, it has been generally held, should either take their subject matter from some mythology, or else should be about some remote historical period, far enough away from the present for the characters not to need to be recognisable as human beings, and therefore for them to be licensed to talk in verse. Picturesque period costume renders verse much more acceptable. Furthermore, my play was to be produced for a rather special kind of audience — an audience

of those serious people who go to "festivals" and expect
to have to put up with poetry — though perhaps on
this occasion some of them were not quite prepared
for what they got. And finally it was a religious play,
and people who go deliberately to a religious play at
a religious festival expect to be patiently bored and
to satisfy themselves with the feeling that they have
done something meritorious. So the path was made
easy.

It was only when I put my mind to thinking what
sort of a play I wanted to do next, that I realised that
in *Murder in the Cathedral* I had not solved any general problem; that from my point of view the play was
a dead end. For one thing, the problem of language
which that play had presented to me was a special
problem. Fortunately, I did not have to write in the
idiom of the twelfth century, because that idiom, even
if I knew Norman French and Anglo-Saxon, would
have been unintelligible. But the vocabulary and style
could not be exactly those of modern conversation — as
in some modern French plays using the plot and personages of Greek drama — because I had to take my

audience back to an historical event; and they could not afford to be archaic, first because archaism would only have suggested the wrong period, and second because I wanted to bring home to the audience the contemporary relevance of the situation. The style therefore had to be *neutral*, committed neither to the present nor to the past. As for the versification, I was only aware at this stage that the essential was to avoid any echo of Shakespeare, for I was persuaded that the primary failure of nineteenth-century poets when they wrote for the theatre (and most of the greatest English poets had tried their hand at drama) was not in their theatrical technique, but in their dramatic language; and that this was due largely to their limitation to a strict blank verse which, after extensive use for nondramatic poetry, had lost the flexibility which blank verse must have if it is to give the the effect of conversation. The rhythm of regular blank verse had become too remote from the movement of modern speech. Therefore what I kept in mind was the versification of *Everyman*, hoping that anything unusual in the sound of it would be on the whole, advantageous. An avoidance of too much iambic, some use of alliteration, and occasional unexpected rhyme, helped to distinguish the versification from that of the nineteenth century.

The versification of the dialogue in *Murder in the Cathedral* has therefore, in my opinion, only a *negative* merit: it succeeded in avoiding what had to be avoided, but it arrived at no positive novelty; in short, in so far as it solved the problem of speech in verse for writing today, it solved it for this play only, and provided me with no clue to the verse I should use in another kind of play. Here, then, were two problems left unsolved: that of the idiom and that of the metric (it is really one and the same problem) for general use in any play I might want to write in future. I next became aware of my reasons for depending, in that play, so heavily upon the assistance of the chorus. There were two reasons for this, which in the circumstances justified it. The first was that the essential action of the play — both the historical facts and the matter which I invented — was somewhat limited. A man comes home, foreseeing that he will be killed, and he is killed. I did not want to increase the number of characters, I did not want to write a chronicle of twelfth-century politics, nor did I want to tamper unscrupulously with the meagre records as Tennyson did (in introducing Fair Rosamund, and in suggesting that Becket had been crossed in love in early youth). I wanted to concentrate on death and martyrdom. The introduction of a chorus of excited and sometimes hysterical women, reflecting in their emotion the significance of the action, helped wonderfully. The second reason was this: that a poet writing for the first time for the stage is much more at home in choral verse than in dramatic dialogue. This, I felt sure, was something I could do, and perhaps the dramatic weaknesses would be somewhat covered up by the cries of the women. The use of a chorus strengthened the power and concealed the defects of my theatrical technique. For this reason I decided that next time I would try to integrate the chorus more closely into the play.

I wanted to find out, also, whether I could learn to dispense altogether with the use of prose. I have already given the justification of this aim. The two prose passages in *Murder in the Cathedral* could not have been written in verse. Certainly, with the kind of dialogue verse which I used in that play, the audience would have been uncomfortably aware that it was verse they were hearing. A sermon cast in verse is too unusual an experience for even the most regular churchgoer: nobody could have responded to it as a sermon at all. And in the speeches of the knights, who are quite aware that they are addressing an audience of people living eight hundred years after they themselves are dead, the use of platform prose is intended of course to have a special effect: to shock the audience out of their complacency. But this is a kind of trick: that is, a device tolerable only in one play and of no use for any other. I may, for aught I know, have been slightly under the influence of *St. Joan*.

I do not wish to give you the impression that I would rule out of dramatic poetry these three things: historical or mythological subject matter, the chorus, and traditional blank verse. I do not wish to lay down any law that the only suitable characters and situations are those of modern life, or that a verse play should consist of dialogue only, or that a wholly new versification is necessary. I am only tracing out the route of exploration of one writer, and that one myself. If the poetic drama is to reconquer its place, it must, in my opinion, enter into overt competition with prose drama. As I have said, people are prepared to put up with verse from the lips of personages dressed in the fashion of some distant age; they should be made to hear it from people dressed like ourselves, living in houses and apartments like ours, and using telephones and motor cars and radio sets. Audiences are prepared to accept poetry recited by a chorus, for that is a kind of poetry recital, which it does them credit to enjoy. And audiences (those who go to a verse play because it is in verse) expect poetry to be in rhythms which have lost touch with colloquial speech. What we have to do is to bring poetry into the world in which the audience lives and to which it returns when it leaves the theatre; not to transport the audience into some imaginary world totally unlike their own, an unreal world in which poetry can be spoken. What I should hope might be achieved, by a generation of dramatists having the benefit of our experience, is that the audience should find, at the moment of awareness that it is hearing poetry, that it is saying to itself: "*I* could talk in poetry too!" Then we should not be transported into an artificial world; on the contrary, our own sordid, dreary, daily world would be suddenly illuminated and transfigured.

I was determined, therefore, in my next play to take a theme of contemporary life, with characters of our own time living in our own world. *The Family Reunion* was the result. Here my first concern was the problem of the versification, to find a rhythm close to contemporary speech, in which the stresses could be made to come wherever we should naturally put them, in uttering the particular phrase on the particular occasion. What I worked out is substantially what I have continued to employ: a line of varying length and varying number of syllables, with a caesura and three stresses. The caesura and the stresses may come at different places, almost anywhere in the line; the stresses may be close together or well separated by light syllables, the only rule being that there must be one stress

46

on one side of the caesura and two on the other. In
retrospect, I soon saw that I had given my attention
to versification, at the expense of plot and character.
I had, indeed, made some progress in dispensing with
the chorus; but the device of using four of the minor
personages, representing the Family, sometimes as individual character parts and sometimes collectively as
chorus, does not seem to me very satisfactory. For one
thing, the immediate transition from individual, char-
acterised part to membership of a chorus is asking too
much of the actors: it is a very difficult transition to
accomplish. For another thing, it seemed to me another
trick, one which, even if successful, could not have
been applicable in another play. Furthermore, I had
in two passages used the device of a lyrical duet further isolated from the rest of the dialogue by being
written in shorter lines with only two stresses. These
passages are in a sense "beyond character"; the speakers
have to be presented as falling into a kind of trance-
like state in order to speak them. But they are so remote
from the necessity of the action that they are hardly
more than passages of poetry which might be spoken

by anybody; they are too much like operatic arias. The member of the audience, if he enjoys this sort of thing, is putting up with a suspension of the action in order to enjoy a poetic fantasia: these passages are really less related to the action than are the choruses in *Murder in the Cathedral*. I observed that when Shakespeare, in one of his mature plays, introduces what might seem a purely poetic line or passage, it never interrupts the action, or is out of character, but, on the contrary, in some mysterious way supports both action and character. When Macbeth speaks his so often quoted words beginning

Tomorrow and tomorrow and tomorrow

or when Othello, confronted at night with his angry father-in-law and friends, utters the beautiful line

Keep up your bright swords, for the dew will rust them

we do not feel that Shakespeare has thought of lines which are beautiful poetry and wishes to fit them in somehow, or that he has for the moment come to the end of his dramatic inspiration and has turned to poetry to fill up with. The lines are surprising, and yet they fit in with the character; or else we are compelled to adjust our conception of the character in such a way that the lines will be appropriate to it. The lines spoken by Macbeth reveal the weariness of the weak man who had been forced by his wife to realise his own halfhearted desires and her ambitions, and who, with her death, is left without the motive to continue. The line of Othello expresses irony, dignity, and fearlessness; and incidentally reminds us of the time of night in which the scene takes place. Only poetry could do this; but it is *dramatic* poetry: that is, it does not interrupt but intensifies the dramatic situation.

It was not only because of the introduction of passages which called too much attention to themselves as poetry, and could not be dramatically justified, that I found *The Family Reunion* defective: there were two weaknesses which came to strike me as more serious still. The first was that I had taken far too much of the strictly limited time allowed to a dramatist in presenting a situation, and not left myself enough time, or provided myself with enough material, for developing it in action. I had written what was, on the whole, a good first act; except that for a first act it was much too long. When the curtain rises again, the audience is expecting, as it has a right to expect, that something is going to happen. Instead, it finds itself treated to a further exploration of the background: in other words, to what ought to have been given much earlier if at all. The beginning of the second act presents much the most difficult problem to producer and cast: for the audience's attention is beginning to wander. And then, after what must seem to the audience an interminable time of preparation, the conclusion comes so abruptly that we are, after all, unready for it. This was an elementary fault in mechanics. But the deepest flaw of all was in a failure of adjustment between the Greek story and the modern situation. I should either have stuck closer to Aeschylus or else taken a great deal more liberty with his myth. One evidence of this is the appearance of those ill-fated figures, the Furies. They must, in future, be omitted from the cast, and be understood to be visible only to certain of my characters, and not to the audience. We tried every possible manner of presenting them. We put them on the stage, and they looked like uninvited guests who had strayed in from a fancy-dress ball. We concealed them behind gauze, and they suggested a still out of a Walt Disney film. We made them dimmer, and they looked like shrubbery just outside the window. I have seen other expedients tried: I have seen them signalling from across the garden, or swarming onto the stage like a football team, and they are never right. They never succeed in being either Greek goddesses or modern spooks. But their failure is merely a symptom of the failure to adjust the ancient with the modern. A more serious evidence is that we are left in a divided frame of mind, not knowing whether to consider the play the tragedy of the mother or the salvation of the son. The two situations are not reconciled. I find a confirmation of this in the fact that my sympathies now have come to be all with the mother, who seems to me, except perhaps for the chauffeur, the only complete human being in the play; and my hero now strikes me as an insufferable prig.

Well, I had made some progress in learning how to write the first act of a play, and I had — the one thing of which I felt sure — made a good deal of progress in finding a form of versification and an idiom which would serve all my purposes, without recourse to prose, and be capable of unbroken transition between the most intense speech and the most relaxed dialogue. You will understand, after my making these criticisms of *The Family Reunion*, some of the errors that I endeavoured to avoid in designing *The Cocktail Party*. To begin with, no chorus, and no ghosts. I was still inclined to go to a Greek dramatist for my theme, but I was determined to take this merely as a point of departure, and to conceal the origins so well that nobody would identify them until I pointed them out myself. In this at least I have been successful; for no one of my acquaintance (and no dramatic critics) recognised the source of my story in the *Alcestis* of Euripides. In fact, I have had to go into detailed explanation to convince them — I mean, of course, those who were familiar with the plot of that play — of the genuineness of the inspiration. But those who were at first disturbed by the eccentric behaviour of my unknown guest, and his apparently intemperate habits and tendency to burst into song, have found some consolation after I have called their attention to the behaviour of Heracles in Euripides' play. In the second place, I laid down for myself the ascetic rule to avoid poetry which could not stand the test of strict dramatic utility: with such success, indeed, that it is perhaps an open question whether there is any poetry in the play at all. And finally, I tried to keep in mind that in a play, from time to time, something should happen; that the audience should be kept in the constant expectation that something is going to happen; and that, when it does happen, it should be different, but not too different, from what the audience has been led to expect.

I have not yet got to the end of my investigation of the weaknesses of this play, but I hope and expect to find more than those of which I am yet aware. I say "hope" because while one can never repeat a success, and therefore must always try to find something different, even if less popular, to do, the desire to write something which will be free of the defects of one's last work is a very powerful and useful incentive. I am aware that the last act of my play only just escapes, if indeed it does escape, the accusation of being not a last act but an epilogue; and I am determined to do something different, if I can, in this respect. I also believe that while the self-education of a poet trying to write for the theatre seems to require a long period of disciplining his poetry, and putting it, so to speak, on a very thin diet in order to adapt it to the needs of the drama, there may be a later stage, when (and if) the understanding of theatrical technique has become second nature, at which he can dare to make more liberal use of poetry and take greater liberties with ordinary colloquial speech. I base that belief on the evolution of Shakespeare, and on some study of the language in his late plays. But to give reason for this belief involves an examination and defense of Shakespeare's late plays as plays; and this obviously is the subject for a separate essay.

In devoting so much time to an examination of my

own plays, I have, I believe, been animated by a better motive than egotism. It seems to me that if we are to have a poetic drama, it is more likely to come from poets learning how to write plays, than from skilful prose dramatists learning to write poetry. That some poets can learn how to write plays, and write good ones, may be only a hope, but I believe a not unreasonable hope; but that a man who has started by writing succesful prose plays should then learn how to write good poetry, seems to me extremely unlikely. And, under present-day conditions, and until the verse play is recognised by the larger public as a possible source of entertainment, the poet is likely to get his first opportunity to work for the stage only after making some sort of reputation for himself as the author of other kinds of verse. I have therefore wished to put on record, for what it may be worth to others, some account of the difficulties I have encountered, and the weaknesses I have had to try to overcome, and the mistakes into which I have fallen.

I should not like to close, however, without attempting to set before myself, and, if I can, before you, though only in dim outline, the ideal towards which it seems to me that poetic drama should strive. It is an unattainable ideal: and that is why it interests me, for it provides an incentive towards further experiment and exploration, beyond any goal which there is prospect of attaining. It is a function of all art to give us some perception of an order in life, by imposing an order upon it. The painter works by selection, combination, and emphasis among the elements of the visible world; the musician, in the world of sound. It seems to me that beyond the nameable, classifiable emotions and motives of our conscious life when directed towards action — the part of life which prose drama is wholly adequate to express — there is a fringe of indefinite extent, of feeling which we can only detect, so to speak, out of the corner of the eye and can never completely focus; of feeling of which we are only aware in a kind of temporary detachment from action. There are great prose dramatists — such as Ibsen and Chekhov — who have at times done things of which I would not otherwise have supposed prose to be capable, but who seem to me, in spite of their success, to have been hampered in expression by writing in prose. This peculiar range of sensibility can be expressed by dramatic poetry, at its moments of greatest intensity. At such moments, we touch the border of those feelings which only music can express. We can never emulate music, because to arrive at the condition of music would be the annihilation of poetry, and especially of dramatic poetry. Nevertheless, I have before my eyes a kind of mirage of the perfection of verse drama, which would be a design of human action and of words, such as to present at once the two aspects of dramatic and of musical order. It seems to me that Shakespeare achieved this at least in certain scenes — even rather early, for there is the balcony scene of *Romeo and Juliet* — and that this was what he was striving towards in his late plays. To go as far in this direction as it is possible to go, without losing that contact with the ordinary everyday world with which drama must come to terms, seems to me the proper aim of dramatic poetry. For it is ultimately the function of art, in imposing a credible order upon ordinary reality, and thereby eliciting some perception of an order *in* reality, to bring us to a condition of serenity, stillness, and reconciliation; and then leave us, as Virgil left Dante, to proceed toward a region where that guide can avail us no further.